1

CW00919226

Message
and Devotion

Revised Edition

with
Selected Prayers
from the
Diary of
St. Maria Faustina Kowalska

Fr. Seraphim Michalenko, MIC
with Vinny Flynn
and Robert A. Stackpole

MARIAN PRESS
STOCKBRIDGE MA 01263

2008

For this revised edition of
The Divine Mercy Message and Devotion

Ecclesiastical Approval of Very Rev. Walter Dziordz, MIC, Provincial Superior of St. Stanislaus Kostka Province of the Marians of the Immaculate Conception, Stockbridge, MA.

For texts from the English Edition of
Diary of St. Maria Faustina Kowalska:

NIHIL OBSTAT:
† George H. Pearce, SM
Former Archbishop of Suva, Fiji

IMPRIMATUR:
† Joseph F. Maguire
Bishop of Springfield, MA
April 9, 1984

The NIHIL OBSTAT and IMPRIMATUR are a declaration that a book or pamphlet is considered to be free from doctrinal or moral error. It is not implied that those who have granted the NIHIL OBSTAT and IMPRIMATUR agree with the contents, opinions or statements expressed.

Front and back cover art of The Divine Mercy and St. Faustina, copyright © Marians of the Immaculate Conception.

Inside art and photos: All copyright © Marians of the Immaculate Conception, except photo on page 6 by Arturo Man and photos on page 21 by *L'Osservatore Romano.*

Library of Congress Catalog Card Number: 2001089908
ISBN: 978-0-944203-47-7

Printed in the United States of America

DECLARATION

In accordance with the decrees of Pope Urban VIII, we wish to state that only private and human faith is attributed to the revelations, extraordinary graces, and incidents that arc described in this booklet. We declare our faithfulness to Holy Mother Church and her judgments in all the matters contained herein. Our desire is to offer the faithful an opportunity to believe in matters that are considered helpful for salvation.

After scrupulously examining the writings of Sr. Maria Faustina Kowalska and finding them without significant error, the Church declared her heroic virtues. With the required miracles, Pope John Paul II then beatified (1993) and canonized (2000) her. At her canonization, he also drew on the insight from her writings that the "Feast of Mercy" should be instituted, stating: "It is important that we accept the whole message that comes to us from the word of God on this Second Sunday of Easter, which from now on throughout the Church, will be called 'Divine Mercy Sunday.' "

In private revelations like those given to St. Faustina, no new doctrine is offered, as Fr. Karl Rahner, SJ, explains in *Theological Investigations* (Vol. 3, pp. 338-339). But they do provide extraordinary guidance for the Church in a time of great and important need. In this case, Pope John Paul II said at St. Faustina's canonization: "By this act, I intend to pass this message on to the new millennium." In that light, we believe *now is the time for mercy.*

TABLE OF CONTENTS

Deeds of Mercy.............................Inside Front Cover
Pope John Paul II at the Tomb of St. Faustina 7
Introduction.. 8

Chapter One: The Story of the Message and Devotion
The Apostle of Mercy 13
The Spread of the Message and Devotion 16

Chapter Two: The Essentials of Divine Mercy
God Is Mercy 25
The ABC's of Mercy 28
  Ask for His Mercy.. 29
  Be Merciful to Others 31
  Completely Trust in Jesus 33

Chapter Three: Experiencing Divine Mercy
The Church: Dispenser of Mercy.. 37
Proclaiming Mercy.. 38
Eucharist: The Presence of Mercy 40
Reconciliation: The Tribunal of Mercy............................ 43
Prayer: The Plea for Mercy 45
Mary, Mother of Mercy.. 49

Chapter Four: Elements of the Message and Devotion
The Image of the Divine Mercy... 52
The Feast of Mercy (Divine Mercy Sunday) 54
The Chaplet of Divine Mercy 63
  How to Recite the Chaplet 65
  How to Sing the Chaplet... 68

The Novena to The Divine Mercy 69
The Hour of Great Mercy 79
Mercy Stations 82
Living the Message of Mercy 83
Mercy for the Dying... 85
Mercy for the Dead 86
Preparing for the Second Coming.............................. 87

Chapter Five: Selected Prayers from the Diary
Little Prayers for use at the Hour of Great Mercy 89
At the Feet of Christ in the Eucharist........................... 89
Praises of The Divine Mercy 91
To The Divine Mercy.. 93
In Thanksgiving 94
To the Mother of God 94
For the Grace to Be Merciful to Others 95
Prayer for the Intercession of
    St. Faustina..Inside Back Cover

On June 7, 1997, Pope John Paul II prays at the tomb of [St.] Faustina in Lagiewniki, Poland.

POPE JOHN PAUL II AT THE TOMB OF ST. FAUSTINA

Pope John Paul II visited the tomb of St. Maria Faustina Kowalska in Lagiewniki, Poland, on June 7, 1997. There he said:

There is nothing that man needs more than Divine Mercy — that love which is benevolent, which is compassionate, which raises man above his weakness to the infinite heights of the holiness of God.

In this place, we become particularly aware of this. From here, in fact, went out the message of Divine Mercy that Christ Himself chose to pass on to our generation through [St.] Faustina.

And it is a message that is clear and understandable for everyone. Anyone can come here, look at this image of the merciful Jesus, His Heart radiating peace, and hear in the depths of his own soul what [St.] Faustina heard: **Fear nothing; I am always with you** *(Diary of St. Maria Faustina Kowalska, 586). And if this person responds with a sincere heart, "Jesus, I trust in You," he will find comfort in all his anxieties and fears. ...*

I come here to commend the concerns of the Church and of humanity to the merciful Christ. On the threshold of the third millennium, I come to entrust to Him once more my Petrine ministry — "Jesus, I trust in You!"

INTRODUCTION

This booklet presents the message of The Divine Mercy and the special forms of devotion to The Divine Mercy that are outlined in the *Diary of St. Faustina.* First published in 1981, the booklet has undergone several revisions over the years, including changes in its title and contents. It has become known throughout the world as the "Devotion Booklet."

Devotion and Devotions

"Devotion," in the root sense of the word, means consecration ... giving of oneself completely ... dedication by solemn vow. In a religious context, devotion is an attitude of caring about God and all that God cares about. It involves a decision and a commitment that permeates our lives, giving direction and form to all our actions.

Among these actions are what we call "devotions": specific religious attitudes, prayers, and practices that express and nurture our devotion — our total consecration to God. Thus, devotions can be of very real value, both as a witness to others and as a fruitful way of growing in personal holiness.

The Constitution on the Sacred Liturgy, presented by the Second Vatican Council, teaches that popular devotions of the Christian people are warmly commended as long as they are in accord with the laws and norms of the Church.

A New Focus on Mercy

From the diary of a young Polish nun, named Sr. Faustina Kowalska, a special devotion to the mercy of God is spreading throughout the world.

The message is nothing new, just a reminder of what the Church has always taught: that God is merciful and forgiving and that we, too, must show mercy and forgiveness.

But, in the Divine Mercy devotion, the message takes on a powerful new focus, calling people to a deeper understanding that God's love is unlimited and available to everyone — especially the greatest sinners: **The greater the sinner, the greater the right he has to My mercy** *(Diary,* 723).

Some of the elements of this new focus include a sacred image of the merciful Savior, several new prayers, and a cornucopia of promises. But the main elements are trust and deeds of mercy.

Devotion to The Divine Mercy involves a total commitment to God as Mercy. It is a decision to accept His mercy with thanksgiving, to trust completely in Him, and to be merciful as He is merciful.

The devotional practices proposed in the *Diary of St. Faustina* and set forth in this booklet are completely in accordance with the teachings of the Church and are firmly rooted in the Gospel message of our Merciful Savior. Properly understood and implemented, they will help us grow as genuine followers of Christ.

"Lip Service" or Merciful Heart?

There are two scriptural verses that we should keep in mind as we involve ourselves in these devotional practices:

1. "This people honors me with their lips, but their hearts are far from me" (Is 29:13);

2. "Blessed are the merciful, for they shall obtain mercy"(Mt 5:7).

Which of these would you and I like to hear the Lord say about us?

It's an ironic and somewhat frightening fact that many of the most religious people of Christ's time (people who were actively practicing their religion and eagerly awaiting the promised Messiah) were not able to recognize Him when He came.

The Pharisees, to whom Christ was speaking in the first quotation above, were very devoted to the prayers, rules, and rituals of their religion; but over the years, these outer observances had become so important in themselves that their real meaning had been lost. The Pharisees performed all the prescribed sacrifices, said all the right prayers, fasted regularly, and talked a lot about God, but none of it had touched their hearts. As a result, they had no real relationship with God, they were not living the way He wanted them to live, and they were not prepared for the coming of Jesus.

When we look at the Image of the Merciful Savior, or pause for prayer at three o'clock, or pray the Chaplet — are these things drawing us closer to the real sacramental life of the Church and allowing Jesus to transform our hearts? Or have they just become religious habits? In our daily lives are we growing more and more as people of mercy? Or are we just giving "lip service" to God's mercy?

Asking for the Lord's mercy, *trusting* in His mercy, and sincerely *trying to live His mercy* in our lives, we can be assured that we will never hear Him say of us, "Their hearts are far from Me," but rather that wonderful promise, "Blessed are the merciful, for they shall obtain mercy."

It is our hope that you will read and reread this booklet and make the prayers, attitudes, and practices presented in it a real part of your life. May you come to trust completely in God and live each day immersed in His merciful love — thus fulfilling the Lord's command to let your light "shine before people, so that they will see the good things you do and praise your Father in heaven" (Mt 5:16).

A lifelike portrait of the Apostle of Mercy sharing The Divine Mercy with a sinful world. The portrait was painted by the renowned artist Janis Balabon under the direction of Fr. Seraphim Michalenko, MIC.

CHAPTER ONE

THE STORY OF THE MESSAGE AND DEVOTION

The origin and spreading of the Divine Mercy message and devotion throughout the world makes for great reading — extraordinary visions and revelations, miraculous answers to prayer, a dramatic escape from war-torn Poland, a temporary ban by the Church, and strong support from Pope John Paul II, who has gone down in history as the "Mercy Pope."

The writings of St. Faustina, an uneducated Polish nun from the Congregation of Sisters of Our Lady of Mercy in Poland, provide the source of the message and devotion presented in this booklet.

In the 1930s, in obedience to her spiritual director, Sr. Faustina wrote a diary of some 600 pages recording the revelations she was receiving about God's mercy.

The Apostle of Mercy

Turning to the saint's early life, she was born Helen Kowalska on August 25, 1905, in Glogowiec, Poland, to a poor, religious family. Helen was the third of 10 children and was baptized in the parish church of Swince Warckie. From a very tender age, she was known for her love of prayer, diligence and obedience, and concern for the poor.

She was called to the religious life during a vision of the suffering Christ. Then, on August 1, 1925, she entered the Congregation of the Sisters of Our Lady of Mercy and took the name Sr. Maria Faustina of the Most Blessed Sacrament. She lived as a member of the Congregation for 13 years, residing in Cracow, Plock, and Vilnius, where she worked as a cook, gardener, and porter.

Externally nothing revealed her rich, mystical interior life. She zealously performed her tasks and faithfully observed the rule of religious life. She was recollected, yet very natural, serene, and full of kindness with disinterested love for her neighbor. Although her life was apparently insignificant and monotonous, she hid within herself an extraordinary union with God.

The mystery of God's mercy, which she contemplated in the word of God as well as in her everyday activities, forms the basis of her spirituality. By contemplating and getting to know the mystery of God's mercy, she developed the attitude of childlike trust in God and of mercy towards her neighbor.

Sister Faustina was also a faithful daughter of the Church. Conscious of her role in the Church, she co-operated with God's mercy in the task of saving poor sinners. At the specific request of the Lord Jesus and following His example, she made a sacrifice of her own life for the sake of sinners. Her spiritual life was distinguished as well by a deep love of the Holy Eucharist and a special devotion to Mary as the Mother of Mercy.

The years she spent in the convent were filled with extraordinary gifts, such as revelations, visions, hidden stigmata, participation in the Passion of the Lord, bilocation, the reading of human souls, prophecy, and the rare gift of mystical espousal and marriage. Her relationship with God, the Blessed Mother, the angels, the saints, the souls in purgatory — with the entire supernatural world — was as real for her as the world she perceived with the senses.

The Lord chose Sr. Faustina as the Apostle and Secretary of His mercy, so she would share the urgent message of Divine Mercy with our troubled modern world. Her mission consisted in three main tasks:

- Reminding the world and the Church of the truth of God's mercy for every human being, as revealed in the Holy Scriptures;

- Entreating Divine Mercy for the whole world, especially for poor sinners, through the practice of new forms of devotion to The Divine Mercy, which are explained in this booklet;

- Initiating the apostolic movement of Divine Mercy, the followers of which proclaim and entreat Divine Mercy for the world and strive to practice the works of mercy following the example of Sr. Faustina.

Sister Faustina recorded the various aspects of her mission in a diary, which she kept at the specific request of her confessor and spiritual director, Fr. Michael Sopocko, and later at the command of the Lord Jesus Himself. In it, she faithfully wrote down all of the Lord's wishes and described the encounters between her soul and Him.

Consumed by tuberculosis and innumerable sufferings, which she offered for poor sinners, Sr. Faustina died in Cracow at the age of 33 on October 5, 1938. Her mortal remains rest at the Shrine of The Divine Mercy in Lagiewniki near Cracow.

Yet, even before her death in 1938, the devotion to The Divine Mercy as revealed in her diary had begun to spread. During the tragic war years of 1939-1945, this devotion grew in strength as people throughout Poland and Lithuania turned to the merciful Savior for comfort and hope.

The Spread of the Message and Devotion

In 1941, the devotion was brought to the USA from Poland by Father Joseph Jarzebowski, a member of the Congregation of Marians of the Immaculate Conception. Father Jarzebowski had at first been skeptical about the great graces received by those who entrusted themselves to The Divine Mercy. But, in the spring of 1940, he vowed that if he were able to safely reach his fellow Marians in America, he would spend the rest of his life spreading the Divine Mercy message and devotion.

After an extraordinary journey from Poland into Lithuania, then across Russia and Siberia to Vladivostok, and from there to Japan, he arrived on American soil a year later. True to his vow, he immediately began distributing information about the message and devotion, with the help of the Felician Sisters in Michigan and Connecticut. His Marian confreres soon became intensely involved as well. After several years of this activity, Fr. Walter Pelczynski, MIC, established in 1944 the "Mercy of God Apostolate" on Eden Hill in Stockbridge, MA, now home of the National Shrine of The Divine Mercy and the Marian Helpers Center, a modern, religious publishing house that has become the international center for the Divine Mercy message and devotion. By 1953, some 25 million pieces of Divine Mercy literature had been distributed around the world.

Banned by the Church

Then, in 1958 and 1959, Sister Faustina's prophecy about the apparent destruction of the Divine Mercy work {*Diary*, 378) began to be fulfilled. The Holy See, having received erroneous and confusing translations *of Diary* entries, which it was unable to verify due to existing political conditions, forbade the spreading of the Divine Mercy message and devotion in the forms proposed by Sister Faustina's writings.

During the period of the ban, the Marians continued to spread devotion to God's mercy, but, in obedience to Rome, they based the message and devotion regarding Divine Mercy on Sacred Scripture, the Liturgy, the teachings of the Church, and Our Lady's revelations at Fatima.

The Lifting of the Ban

Twenty years later (in 1978), the ban was completely lifted, thanks to the intervention of the Archbishop of Krakow, Cardinal Karol Wojtyla. Through his efforts, an Informative Process relating to the life and virtues of Sister Faustina was begun in 1965. Its successful outcome led to the inauguration of her Beatification Cause in 1968.

In a new "Notification" on April 15, 1978, the Sacred Congregation for the Doctrine of the Faith, having reviewed many original documents that were not made available to it in 1959, reversed its earlier decision and declared the 1959 prohibition "no longer binding."

Six months later, Cardinal Karol Wojtyla became Pope John Paul II.

Prompted by the pastoral concern of His Excellency, Joseph F. Maguire, Bishop of Springfield, Massachusetts, with regard to the resuming of efforts to make the Divine Mercy message and devotion known, the Congregation of Marians asked for an authoritative explanation of the Notification of 1978. On July 12, 1979, they received a reply from the Prefect of the Sacred Congregation, stating that "there no longer exists, on the part of this Sacred Congregation, any impediment to the spreading of the devotion to The Divine Mercy in the authentic forms proposed by the Religious Sister mentioned above [Sister Faustina Kowalska]."

Thus, in 1979 — with the local bishop's permission — the Marians resumed their work of spreading the Divine Mercy message and devotion in the forms proposed by Sr. Faustina. The response from laity, priests, and bishops all over the world has been overwhelming, and the devotion has grown faster than anyone ever expected.

Pope John Paul II

One of the reasons for this was certainly the continued support of Pope John Paul II. In 1981, he published an encyclical letter entitled *Rich in Mercy,* in which he speaks of Christ as the "incarnation of mercy ... the inexhaustible source of mercy" (8). He goes on to emphasize that "Christ's messianic program, the program of mercy" must become "the program of His people, the program of the Church" (8).

Throughout the encyclical, John Paul stresses that the Church — especially in our modern times — has the "right and the duty" to "profess and proclaim God's mercy," to "introduce it and make it incarnate" in the lives of all people, and "to call upon the mercy of God," imploring it for the whole world. (See *Rich in Mercy* 12-15.)

A year after publishing *Rich in Mercy*, Pope John Paul II visited the Shrine of Merciful Love in Collevalenza, Italy, during his first pilgrimage outside Rome after the attempt on his life. There he emphasized that spreading the message of mercy was his "special task."

Beatification

On April 18, 1993, Pope John Paul II beatified Sr. Faustina at St. Peter's Square in Rome. It was the first Sunday after Easter — the very day that is to be celebrated as Divine Mercy Sunday, according to the Merciful Savior's revelations to Sr. Faustina. And it was precisely John Paul II who beatified her, the very one who had initiated the Informative Process for her cause in 1965 when he was Archbishop of Cracow, Poland.

In his homily, John Paul said: "I salute you, Sr. Faustina. Beginning today the Church calls you Blessed ... . O Faustina, how extraordinary your life is! Precisely you, the poor and simple daughter of Mazovia, of the Polish people, were chosen by Christ to remind people of this great mystery of Divine Mercy! You bore this mystery within yourself, leaving this world after a short life, filled with suffering. However, at the same time, this mystery has become a prophetic reminder to the world ....

" 'I feel certain that my mission will not come to an end upon my death, but will begin ... ,' Sr. Faustina wrote in her diary *(Diary,* 281). And it truly did! Her mission continues and is yielding astonishing fruit. It is truly marvelous how her devotion to the merciful Jesus is spreading in our contemporary world and gaining so many human hearts! This is undoubtedly a sign of the times — a sign of our 20th century. The balance of this century which is now ending, in addition to the advances which have often surpassed those of preceding eras, presents a deep restlessness and fear of the future. Where, if not in The Divine Mercy, can the world find refuge and the light of hope? Believers understand that perfectly."

Canonization

Then, on April 30, 2000, Pope John Paul H canonized Sr. Faustina as the first saint of the Great Jubilee Year. And again, it was on Divine Mercy Sunday, hi fact, the Holy Father also announced during his homily that the Second Sunday of Easter would now be celebrated as Divine Mercy Sunday throughout the universal Church.

In his homily, John Paul said: "Today my joy is truly great in presenting the life and witness of Sr. Faustina Kowalska to the whole Church as a gift of God for our time. By Divine Providence, the life of this humble daughter of Poland was completely linked with the history of the 20th century, the century we have just left behind. ...

"In fact, it was between the First and Second World Wars that Christ entrusted His message of mercy to her. Those who remember, who were witnesses and participants in the events of those years and the horrible sufferings they caused for millions of people, know well how necessary was the message of mercy.

"Jesus told Sr. Faustina: **Mankind will not have peace until it turns with trust to My mercy** (*Diary,* 300). Through the work of the Polish religious, this message has become linked forever to the 20th century, the last of the second millennium and the bridge to the third. It is not a new message but can be considered a gift of special enlightenment that helps us to relive the Gospel of Easter more intensely, to offer it as a ray of light to the men and women of our time.

"What will the years ahead bring us? ... We are not given to know. ... But the light of Divine Mercy, which the Lord in a way wished to return to the world through Sr. Faustina's charism, will illumine the way for the men and women of the third millennium. ... Sr. Faus-

The banner at St. Faustina's canonization in Rome, April 30, 2000.
Inset: His Holiness reads the words of canonization.

tina's canonization has a particular eloquence: by this act I intend today to pass this message on to the new millennium. ..."

Now, inspired by the legacy of the Mercy Pope, it is our task to spread the message of Divine Mercy in the third millennium.

CHAPTER TWO

THE ESSENTIALS OF DIVINE MERCY

Divine Mercy is the heart of the Gospel. If we really look at how God has revealed Himself in Scripture and Church Tradition, we discover afresh how mercy is essential to understanding His message of love and salvation. Mercy even reveals His very identity. With this understanding of God and His revelation to us, we can ask for His mercy, be merciful to others, and strive to completely trust in His Son, who is Divine Mercy Incarnate.

God Is Mercy

The merciful love of God is the central theme of the Bible. In the Old Testament, God solemnly declared to Moses that He is "a God merciful and gracious, slow to anger, and abounding in steadfast love and faithfulness" (Ex 34:6). In fact, the whole story of God's Chosen People, Israel, shows how the Lord taught them more and more of His faithfulness to His merciful love for them, and His compassion for their plight. As Pope John Paul II wrote in his encyclical *Rich in Mercy:* "In the course of [Israel's] history, this people continuously entrusted itself, both when stricken with misfortune and when it became aware of its sin, to the God of mercies" (4).

The New Testament further develops this message of the merciful love of God. Saint John tells us that God "so loved the world that He gave His only begotten Son, that whoever believes in Him should not perish but have eternal life" (Jn 3:16).

The mercy of God was especially shown when the Son of God gave His life for us on the cross, "while we were yet sinners" (Rom 5:8). Then He rose again in glory to be with us always and to give us the hope of everlasting life. That is why we can declare with great confidence: "Blessed be the God and Father of our Lord Jesus! By His great mercy, we have been born anew to a living hope through the resurrection of Jesus Christ from the dead, and to an inheritance which is imperishable, undefiled, and unfading, kept in heaven for you" (1 Pt 1:3-4).

Throughout the Church's Tradition, the merciful love of God is a constant refrain, echoing the Scriptures. The great Church Fathers St. Augustine and St. Thomas Aquinas taught that in God's relationship with His creatures, mercy is His greatest attribute. Jesus said the same to St. Faustina (see *Diary*, 180 and 301). This truth is also developed in teachings of Pope John Paul II (see *Rich in Mercy*, 14).

The great mystic St. Catherine of Siena found the mercy of God expressed through all of His acts of creation and redemption, so that she finally exclaimed, "O

Mercy! My heart is engulfed with the thought of You! For wherever I turn my thoughts, I find nothing but Mercy!" *(The Dialogue,* 30).

What then is the meaning of Divine "Mercy"? God's very nature is love (see Jn 4:8): infinite, eternal, self-giving love among the Father, the Son, and the Holy Spirit. But "mercy" is the form that God's love takes when it overflows His divine life and pours out upon His creatures. This *Divine Mercy is compassionate love* — a love that seeks to meet the needs and relieve the miseries of others.

Recognizing our human weaknesses and sins, God is always ready to pour out His mercy upon us. Father George Kosicki, CSB, expresses this well in his book *Now Is the Time for Mercy:*

"Mercy, then, is God's love poured out upon us; it is when God, who is love itself, loves us. This flowing quality of mercy is most dramatically represented by Christ on the cross as, through the Blood and Water gushing forth from His pierced Heart, He pours His very life out as a fountain of mercy for us ... . And we also find it in the great chant of the Church, the *Kyrie Eleison* ('Lord, have mercy'), which for centuries has resounded throughout the world at every celebration of the Eucharist and the Liturgy of Hours. The word *eleison,* which in Greek means 'have mercy,' has the root meaning of 'oil being poured out,' so whenever we say,

'Lord, have mercy,' we are really saying, 'Lord, pour Your love out upon us, pour Yourself out upon us' " (Marian Press, 1993).

We find the very same message echoing like a refrain throughout the *Diary of St. Faustina.* Jesus said to her:

I am Love and Mercy itself (1074). **My Heart overflows with great mercy for souls, and especially for poor sinners ... it is for them that the Blood and Water flowed from my Heart as from a fount overflowing with mercy** (367). **Let no soul fear to draw near to Me, even though its sins be as scarlet** (699). **My mercy is greater than your sins, and those of the entire world** (1485). **I let my Sacred Heart be pierced with a lance, thus opening wide the source of mercy for you. Come then with trust to draw graces from this fountain** (1485).

The ABC's of Mercy

We have just seen that God is Love and Mercy itself. The message of mercy is that God loves us — all of us, no matter how great our sins. He wants us to recognize that His mercy is greater than our sins, so that we will call upon Him with trust, receive His mercy, and let it flow through us to others. Thus, all will come to share His joy. It is a message we can call to mind simply by remembering ABC.

*A*sk for His Mercy. God wants us to approach Him in prayer constantly, repenting of our sins and asking Him to pour His mercy out upon us and upon the whole world.

*B*e Merciful to Others. God wants us to receive His mercy and let it flow through us to others. He wants us to extend love and forgiveness to others just as He does to us.

*C*ompletely Trust in Jesus. God wants us to know that the graces of His mercy are dependent upon our trust. The more we trust in Jesus, the more we will receive.

Ask for His Mercy

Through the passion and death of Jesus, an infinite ocean of mercy was made available for all of us. But God, who created us free, will not force anything on us, not even His mercy. He must wait for us to turn from our sinfulness and ask:

"Ask and it will be given to you ... for everyone who asks receives" (Mt 7:7, 8).

The Scriptures are filled with examples of how to trust in God and ask for His mercy: the psalms; the faith of Abraham and Moses who pleaded and "bargained" with God; the man who persuaded his friend to get up in the middle of the night to lend him some bread; the persistent widow who secured justice from the unjust judge; the Canaanite woman who "argued" with Jesus about her right to His mercy; and the witness of Mary, whose appeal for mercy at Cana led Jesus to perform His first public miracle, thus acknowledging that His time had indeed come.

Pope John Paul II echoes this scriptural message with a new urgency for our own times:

"At no time ... especially at a moment as critical as our own — can the Church forget the prayer that is a cry for the mercy of God. ... The Church has the right and the duty to appeal to the God of mercy 'with loud cries' " *(Rich in Mercy,* 15).

To St. Faustina, Jesus revealed this same message once again. He gave her three new ways to ask for mercy on the strength of His passion: the Chaplet, the Novena, and prayer at three o'clock; and He taught her to transform her daily life into a continuous prayer for mercy. Through her, He calls us all to ask for His mercy:

Souls that make an appeal to My mercy delight Me. To such souls I grant even more graces than they ask. I cannot punish even the greatest sinner if he makes an appeal to My compassion *(Diary,* 1146). **Beg for mercy for the whole world** (570). **No soul that has called upon My mercy has ever been disappointed** (1541).

Be Merciful to Others

Mercy is love that seeks to relieve the misery of others. It is an active love, poured out upon others to heal, to comfort, to console, to forgive, to remove pain. It is the love that God offers us, and it is the love He demands from us for each other:

"I give you a new commandment. ... As I have loved you, so you must love one another" (Jn 13:34). "Be merciful, even as your Father is merciful" (Lk 6:36).

A work of mercy: Fr. Stanislaus Chryc, MIC, delivers food and treats to poor children in Poland.

Repeatedly the Scriptures remind us that the measure we use for others is the measure God will use for us (Lk 6:38), for He will indeed "forgive us our trespasses as we forgive those who trespass against us" (Mt 6:12-14). "Blessed are the merciful, for they shall obtain mercy" (Mt 5:7), but "judgment is without mercy to one who has shown no mercy" (Jas 2:13). The parables of the Good Samaritan, the Rich Man and Lazarus, and the Unforgiving Servant all demonstrate this essential truth that only if we give mercy can we hope to receive it; for we will be judged on the basis of our merciful actions toward others: "I was hungry and you gave me food ..." (Mt 25:35-46).

Our Lord spoke to St. Faustina about the importance of deeds of mercy on several occasions.

I demand from you deeds of mercy which are to arise out of love for Me. You are to show mercy to your neighbors always and everywhere. You must not shrink from this or try to excuse yourself from it. ... Even the strongest faith is of no avail without works *(Diary,* 742). **If a soul does not exercise mercy in some way, it will not obtain My mercy on the day of judgment** (1317).

How do we exercise mercy? Through our actions, our words, and our prayers, by performing the Spiritual and Corporal Works of Mercy [see the inside cover of this booklet], and by developing an attitude of mercy in our daily lives. Every day we can choose to respond to the people and events we encounter by immersing them in the ocean of God's mercy. Instead of "cursing the darkness" and despairing over the condition of the world, we bless the world with God's mercy, thus allowing Him to heal it. [See also pages 75-77.]

Completely Trust in Jesus

Trust in Jesus is the essence of the message of mercy. When we go to a public fountain, we can draw water from it as long as we have a vessel or container of some kind to put the water in. If our vessel is small, we can only bring back a little water; if it's large, we can bring back a lot. And anyone with a vessel can draw water from the fountain. The water is there for us, and no one is excluded. All we need is a vessel.

So it is with God's mercy. In repeated revelations to St. Faustina, Our Divine Savior makes it clear that the fountain is His Heart, the water is His mercy, and the vessel is trust.

I have opened My Heart as a living fountain of mercy. Let all souls draw life from it. Let them approach this sea of mercy with great trust (*Diary*, 1520). **On the cross, the fountain of My mercy was opened wide by the lance for all souls — no one have I excluded!** (1182). **I am offering people a vessel with which they are to keep coming for graces to the**

fountain of mercy. **That vessel is this image with the signature: "Jesus, I trust in You"** (327). **The graces of My mercy are drawn by means of one vessel only, and that is — trust. The more a soul trusts, the more it will receive** (1578).

In the *Diary of St. Faustina*, we hear Our Lord reminding us that we can depend upon His love ... that He alone is worthy of our trust:

I never reject a contrite heart (1485). **Sooner would heaven and earth turn into nothingness than would My mercy not embrace a trusting soul** (1777).

But there is more to trust than just believing that God is trustworthy. We have to act upon that belief. Trust involves a turning back to God, a real conversion of our whole lives to God, repenting of our sins and forgiving others. Trust is a living faith.

Trust means that we agree to let God be God, instead of trying to be God ourselves. (Trust is the antidote to the first sin of Adam!) It means that we agree that God can write the script of our lives, instead of insisting on our own script. It means that we agree with the great pledge we make in the Our Father: "Your will [not mine] be done on earth as it is in heaven." It means that even in our moments of agony we agree with the cry of Jesus in the Garden, "Not my will, but Yours be done" (Lk 22:42).

34

God is Mercy itself, and we are called to practice the ABC's of mercy. As we do, our trust in Jesus is the vital ingredient. We don't simply ask for mercy, nor do we simply try to be good to other people. We ask with complete trust, and Our Lord fills us with grace so that we can be merciful as our Heavenly Father is merciful.

I am Love and Mercy itself. When a soul approaches Me with trust, I fill it with such an abundance of graces that it cannot contain them within itself, but radiates them to other souls (1074).

The Sisters of Our Lady of Mercy in Lagiewniki, Poland, pray at the Hour of Great Mercy.

CHAPTER THREE

EXPERIENCING DIVINE MERCY

We now know Divine Mercy is at the very heart of the Gospel, but how can we experience this mercy in our own lives? Jesus said to St. Faustina: **Tell aching mankind to snuggle close to My merciful Heart, and I will fill it with peace** (*Diary,* 1074). Thus, it is only by drawing near to Jesus Christ — the very Incarnation of Divine Mercy — and trusting in Him that we can fully experience the love and peace of God. And the best place to encounter the merciful love of Jesus Christ is in His Church, which St. Paul calls "the Body of Christ" (1 Cor 12:27).

As we shall see, in the Body of Christ, the Church, we are given a whole "program of mercy." The Church proclaims the mercy of God, and she dispenses the Sacraments of mercy. As the Body of Christ, the Church prays for God's mercy on the whole world. Also, Mary — our Mother of Mercy and Mother of the Church — plays a unique role in God's eternal plan of mercy.

The Church: Dispenser of Mercy

Pope John Paul II teaches in his encyclical *Rich in Mercy* that the whole life and mission of the Church centers upon Jesus, The Divine Mercy, who empowers her to proclaim, practice, and implore mercy:

"Christ's messianic program, the program of mercy, becomes the program of His people, the program of the Church" (8). "The Church proclaims the truth of God's mercy revealed in the crucified and risen Christ, and she professes it in various ways. Furthermore, she seeks to practice mercy towards people through people, and she sees in this an indispensable condition for solicitude for a better and 'more human' world, today and tomorrow" (15). "Finally, the Church — professing mercy and remaining always faithful to it — has the right and duty to call upon the mercy of God, imploring it in the face of all the manifestations of physical and moral evil, before all the threats that cloud the whole horizon of the life of humanity today" (12).

In particular, John Paul emphasizes:

"The Church lives an authentic life when she professes and proclaims mercy — the most stupendous attribute of the Creator and of the Redeemer — and when she brings people close to the source of the Savior's mercy, of which she is the trustee and dispenser [especially through the Sacraments of the Eucharist and Reconciliation]" (13).

Proclaiming Mercy

"The Church," writes Pope John Paul II, "must consider it one of her principal duties — at every stage of history and especially in our modern age — to proclaim and to introduce into life the mystery of mercy supreme-ly revealed in Jesus Christ" *(Rich in Mercy, 14).*

This need to proclaim God's mercy is a constantly recurring theme in the *Diary of St. Faustina:*

Proclaim to the whole world My unfathomable mercy (1142).

Proclaim that mercy is the greatest attribute of God. All the works of My hand are crowned with mercy (301).

Souls who spread the honor of My mercy I shield through their entire life as a tender mother her in-fant, and at the hour of death I will not be a Judge for them, but the Merciful Savior (1075).

Do whatever is within your power to spread devo-tion to My mercy. I will make up for what you lack. Tell aching mankind to snuggle close to My merciful Heart, and I will fill it with peace (1074).

Tell My priests that hardened sinners will repent on hearing their words when they speak about My unfathomable mercy, about the compassion I have for them in My Heart. To priests who proclaim and extol My mercy, I will give wondrous power; I will anoint their words and touch the hearts of those to whom they will speak (1521).

Eucharist: The Presence of Mercy

In His great love for us, the Lord Jesus gave us a great miracle of mercy: the Sacrament of the Holy Eucharist.

God did not only become man in the Incarnation to give His life for us on the cross and to rise again in glory. The Incarnation also looked forward to Jesus remaining with us to the end of time in the Eucharist. By this great miracle of Our Lord's love, the Real Presence of Jesus remains with us under the form of bread and wine. As Pope Paul VI wrote in *The Credo of the People of God*:

"The unique and indivisible existence of the Lord glorious in heaven is rendered present by the sacrament in the many places on earth where the Mass is celebrated. And this existence remains present after the Sacrifice, in the Blessed Sacrament which is, in the tabernacle, the living heart of each of our churches. And it is our very sweet duty to honor and adore in the blessed Host which our eyes see, the Incarnate Word whom they cannot see, and who, without leaving heaven, is made present before us" (pub. 1968).

The Eucharist is central to devotion to The Divine Mercy, and many of the elements of the devotion are essentially Eucharistic — especially the Image, the Chaplet, and the Feast of Mercy. The Image, with its red and pale rays, represents the Eucharistic Lord Jesus, whose

Heart has been pierced and now pours forth blood and water as a fountain of mercy for us. It is the Image of God's sacrificial gift of mercy made present in every Mass.

Several times in her *Diary*, St. Faustina writes of seeing the red and pale rays coming, not from the Image, but from the Sacred Host; and once, as the priest exposed the Blessed Sacrament, she saw the rays from the Image pierce the Host and spread out from it all over the world (see 441). So too, with the eyes of faith, we should see in every Host the merciful Savior pouring Himself out as a fountain of mercy for us.

This concept of the Eucharist as a fountain of grace and mercy is not only found in the *Diary*, but also in Church teaching. The Church clearly teaches that all the other sacraments are directed towards the Eucharist and draw their power from it.

In the Constitution on the Sacred Liturgy, for example, we read: "Especially from the Eucharist, grace is poured forth upon us as from a fountain." And, in a note in the Catechism of the Council of Trent, pastors are urged to "compare the Eucharist to a fountain and the other sacraments to rivulets. For the Holy Eucharist is truly and necessarily to be called the fountain of all graces, containing, as it does, after an admirable manner, the fountain itself of celestial gifts and graces, and

the Author of all the Sacraments, Christ Our Lord, from whom, as from its source, is derived whatever of goodness and perfection the other sacraments possess" (10).

No wonder, then, that St. Faustina was so devoted to the Eucharist and wrote so powerfully about it in her *Diary*:

"Oh what awesome mysteries take place during Mass! ... One day we will know what God is doing for us in each Mass, and what sort of gift He is preparing in it for us. Only His divine love could permit that such a gift be provided for us ... this fountain of life gushing forth with such sweetness and power" (914).

"All the good that is in me is due to Holy Communion" (1392). "Herein lies the whole secret of my sanctity" (1489). "One thing alone sustains me and that is Holy Communion. From it I draw all my strength; in it is all my comfort. ... Jesus concealed in the Host is everything to me. ... I would not know how to give glory to God if I did not have the Eucharist in my heart" (1037).

Reconciliation: The Tribunal of Mercy

To help us prepare to receive within us the actual Body and Blood, Soul and Divinity of our merciful Savior in the Eucharist, Our Lord left us another "miracle of mercy," the Sacrament of Reconciliation. Here, too, Jesus is present for us — for *all* of us, no matter how great our sins — as the merciful Savior, the fountain of mercy that cleanses, comforts, forgives, and restores to life.

When you go to confession, to this fountain of mercy, the Blood and Water which came forth from My Heart always flows down upon your soul *(Diary,* 1602). **[I]n the Tribunal of Mercy** [the Sacrament of Reconciliation] ... **the greatest miracles take place and are incessantly repeated** (1448). **Here the misery of the soul meets the God of mercy** (1602).

Come with faith to the feet of My representative (1448). **I Myself am waiting there for you. I am**

43

only hidden by the priest ... I Myself act in your soul (1602). Make your confession before Me. The person of the priest is, for Me, only a screen. Never analyze what sort of a priest it is that I am making use of; open your soul in confession as you would to Me, and I will fill it with My light (1725).

Were a soul like a decaying corpse, so that from a human standpoint, there would be no hope of restoration and everything would already be lost, it is not so with God. The miracle of Divine Mercy restores that soul in full. Oh, how miserable are those who do not take advantage of the miracle of God's mercy! (1448).

To emphasize the importance of these two great sacraments of mercy, Our Lord has made their reception a necessary condition for obtaining His promise of complete forgiveness of sins and punishment for those observing the Feast of Mercy. [See pages 52-53.] And Pope John Paul II, who repeatedly stressed the importance of God's message of mercy, has exhorted us that, "the Church of the new Advent... must be the Church of the Eucharist and of Penance" *(Redemptor Hominis).*

In her *Diary,* St. Faustina pointed out that the Sacrament of Reconciliation not only obtains for us God's forgiveness, but also heals the soul of the wounds of sin:

"Concerning Holy Confession. We should derive two kinds of profit from Holy Confession:

1. We come to confession to be healed;

2. We come to be educated — like a small child, our soul has constant need of education" (377).

This focus on sacramental confession as a source of spiritual healing is clearly emphasized in the *Catechism of the Catholic Church:*

"The Lord Jesus Christ, physician of our souls and bodies, who forgave the sins of the paralytic and restored him to bodily health, has willed that His Church continue in the power of the Holy Spirit, His work of healing and salvation, even among her own members. This is the purpose of the two sacraments of healing: the Sacrament of Penance [Reconciliation] and the Sacrament of the Anointing of the Sick" (1421). "Indeed the Sacrament of Reconciliation with God brings about a true 'spiritual resurrection,' restoring the dignity and blessings of the children of God, of which the most precious is friendship with God" (1468).

Prayer: The Plea for Mercy

Along with the Sacraments, both corporate and personal prayer is essential if we are to experience God's mercy. True prayer is the dialogue of a trusting soul with the God of mercy. Whether we are confessing our sins in prayer, or giving praise or thanks to God, authentic prayer always springs from our trust in the merciful love of God. It opens us to receive more and more of His love.

Blessed George Matulaitis, the Renovator of the Marians of the Immaculate Conception, provides us with a beautiful example of this kind of prayer in his *Spiritual Journal:*

"Once again, I examined my life. On all sides, I see how corrupt my human nature is. Lord, such weakness. So many imperfections. I would fall into despair if I did not trust so completely in Your infinite mercy.

"I can see, Lord, how Your abundant graces, flowing like the waters of a stream, constantly wash and purify my soul of the dust of its imperfections and the dirt of its transgressions. Thank You for this, O merciful God!"

Intercessory prayer, too, must flow from trust in God's mercy. We do not have to convince God to be merciful to us because — as we have seen — He is "Love and Mercy itself *(Diary,* 1074). He is always ready to pour His merciful love into our hearts if we are only willing to ask and receive Him. Jesus says, "Behold, I stand at the door and knock" (Rev 3:20). Through our humble prayer of petition, we open the door to Him in every circumstance of life. Saint Faustina understood the need for such prayer, especially in difficulties:

"In whatever state a soul may be, it ought to pray. A soul which is pure and beautiful must pray, or else it will lose its beauty; a soul which is striving after this purity must pray, or else it will never attain it; a soul which is newly converted must pray, or else it will fall again; a sinful soul, plunged in sins, must pray so that it might rise again. There is no soul which is not bound to pray, for every single grace comes to the soul through prayer" *(Diary, 146)*.

"Jesus gave me to understand how a soul should be faithful to prayer despite torments, dryness, and temptations; because oftentimes the realization of God's great plans depends mainly on such prayer. If we do not persevere in such prayer, we frustrate what the Lord wanted to do through us or within us" (872).

Our Lady of Guadalupe who told the visionary Juan Diego, "I am a Merciful Mother."

Mary, Mother of Mercy

"Hail Holy Queen, Mother of mercy." For centuries people have invoked Mary under this title, and now, in modern times, Pope John Paul II presented it to us again to emphasize the unique role Mary plays in God's eternal plan of mercy. In his encyclical letter *Rich in Mercy,* he devotes an entire section to Mary, the "Mother of Mercy." She is the one, he explains, who has the deepest understanding of God's mercy, the one who, more than anyone else, deserved and received mercy. Called in a special way to share her Son's mission to reveal His love, she continues to proclaim His mercy "from generation to generation" (9).

For St. Faustina, Mary was a constant source of God's Mercy, as mother, guardian, teacher, and intercessor. From Mary, she received a special gift of purity, strength in suffering, and countless lessons on the spiritual life. "Mary is my Instructress," she writes, "who is ever teaching me how to live for God" {*Diary,* 620). "The more I imitate the Mother of God, the more deeply I get to know God" (843). "[B]efore every Holy Communion, I earnestly ask the Mother of God to help me prepare my soul for the coming of her Son" (1114). "She has taught me how to love God interiorly and also how to carry out His will in all things" (40). "O Mary, my Mother, I place everything in your hands" (79). "O Mary, you are joy, because through you God descended to earth and into my heart" (40).

Jesus, I Trust In You!

The Divine Mercy: The original version of the Image painted under St. Faustina's direction by E. Kazimirowski in 1934. There are now many different versions.

CHAPTER FOUR

ELEMENTS OF THE MESSAGE AND DEVOTION

Through St. Faustina, the merciful Savior has given the aching world new channels for the outpouring of His grace. These new channels include the Image of The Divine Mercy, the Feast of Mercy (Divine Mercy Sunday), the Chaplet, the Novena to The Divine Mercy, and prayer at 3 O'clock in the afternoon, the Hour of Great Mercy. These new channels of mercy are covered first in this chapter.

Although these means of receiving God's mercy are new in form, we shall see that they all proclaim the timeless message of God's merciful love. They also draw us back to the great Sacrament of Mercy, the Holy Eucharist, where the Heart of Jesus overflows with mercy for all. As Jesus told St. Faustina:

My Heart overflows with great mercy for souls, and especially for poor sinners. ... [I]t is for them that the Blood and Water flowed from My Heart as from a fount overflowing with mercy. For them I dwell in the tabernacle as King of Mercy *(Diary, 367)*.

After covering these new channels of mercy, we also touch on some aspects of Church teaching and devotion that are being more deeply appreciated through a greater understanding of Divine Mercy: the Stations of the Cross ("the Mercy Stations"), the corporal and spiritual works of mercy ("Living the Message of Mercy"), praying for the dying ("Mercy for the Dying"), prayer for the Holy Souls in Purgatory ("Mercy for the Dead"), and preparing for the Second Coming (the urgency of proclaiming the message of mercy before Jesus returns).

The Image of The Divine Mercy

In 1931, Our Lord appeared to St. Faustina in a vision. She saw Jesus clothed in a white garment with His right hand raised in blessing. His left hand was touching His garment in the area of the Heart, from where two large rays came forth, one red and the other pale. She gazed intently at the Lord in silence, her soul filled with awe, but also with great joy. Jesus said to her:

Paint an image according to the pattern you see with the signature: Jesus, I trust in You. I promise that the soul that will venerate this image will not perish. I also promise victory over [its] enemies already here on earth, especially at the hour of death. I Myself will defend it as My own glory *(Diary,* 47, 48). **I am offering people a vessel with which they are to keep coming for graces to the fountain of mercy. That vessel is this image with the signature: "Jesus, I trust in You"** (327). **I desire that this image be venerated, first in your chapel, and [then] throughout the world** (47).

At the request of her spiritual director, St. Faustina asked the Lord about the meaning of the rays in the Image. She heard these words in reply:

The two rays denote Blood and Water. The pale ray stands for the Water which makes souls righteous. The red ray stands for the Blood which is the life of souls. These two rays issued forth from the depths of My tender mercy when My agonized Heart was opened by a lance on the Cross.... Happy is the one who will dwell in their shelter, for the just hand of God shall not lay hold of him (299). By means of this image I shall grant many graces to souls. It is to be a reminder of the demands of My mercy, because even the strongest faith is of no avail without works (742).

These words indicate that the Image represents the graces of Divine Mercy poured out upon the world, especially through Baptism and the Eucharist.

Many different versions of this image have been painted, but Our Lord made it clear that the painting itself is not what is important.

When St. Faustina first saw the original image that was being painted under her direction, she wept in disappointment and complained to Jesus: "Who will paint You as beautiful as You are?" (313).

In answer she heard these words:

Not in the beauty of the color, nor of the brush lies the greatness of this image, but in My grace (313).

So, no matter which version of the Image we prefer, we can be assured that it is a vehicle of God's grace if it is revered with trust in His mercy.

The Feast of Mercy

Among all of the elements of devotion to The Divine Mercy requested by Our Lord through Sr. Faustina, the Feast of Mercy holds first place. The Lord's will with regard to its establishment was already made known in His first revelation to the saint. In all, there were 14 revelations concerning the desired feast.

The most comprehensive revelation can be found in *Diary* entry 699: My **daughter, tell the whole world about My inconceivable mercy. I desire that the Feast of Mercy be a refuge and a shelter for all souls, and especially for poor sinners. On that day the very depths of My tender mercy are open. I pour out a whole ocean of graces upon those souls who approach the fount of My mercy.**

The soul that will go to Confession and receive Holy Communion shall obtain complete forgiveness of sins and punishment. On that day are opened all the divine floodgates through which graces flow. Let no soul fear to draw near to Me, even though its sins be as scarlet.

My mercy is so great that no mind, be it of man or of angel, will be able to fathom it throughout all eternity. Everything that exists has come from the very depths of My most tender mercy. Every soul in its relation to Me will contemplate My love and mercy throughout eternity.

The Feast of Mercy emerged from My very depths of tenderness. It is My desire that it be solemnly celebrated on the first Sunday after Easter. Mankind will not have peace until it turns to the Fount of My mercy.

Our Lord's explicit desire is that this feast be celebrated on the first Sunday after Easter. This Sunday is designated in "The Liturgy of the Hours and the Celebration of the Eucharist" as the "Octave Day of Easter." It was officially called the *Second Sunday of Easter* after the liturgical reform of Vatican II. Now, by the Decree of the Congregation for Divine Worship and the Discipline of the Sacraments, the name of this liturgical day has been changed to: "Second Sunday of Easter, or Divine Mercy Sunday."

Pope John Paul II made the surprise announcement of this change in his homily at the canonization of Sr. Faustina on April 30, 2000. There, he declared: "It is important then that we accept the whole message that comes to us from the word of God on this Second Sunday of Easter, which from now on throughout the Church, *will be called 'Divine Mercy Sunday.'* "

By the words "the whole message," Pope John Paul II was referring to the connection between the "Easter Mystery of the Redemption" — in other words, the suffering, death, burial, resurrection, and ascension of Christ, followed by the sending of the Holy Spirit — and this Feast of Divine Mercy, the Octave Day of Easter.

This connection is evident from the scripture readings appointed for this Sunday. As John Paul said, citing the Responsorial Psalm of the Liturgy, "The Church sings ... , as if receiving from Christ's lips these words of the Psalm." "Give thanks to the Lord for He is good; His steadfast love (=mercy) endures forever" (Ps 118:1). And then, Pope John Paul II developed the connection further: "[This comes] from the lips of the risen Christ, who bears the great message of Divine Mercy and entrusts its ministry to the Apostles in the Upper Room: 'Peace be with you. As the Father has sent Me, even so I send you. ... Receive the Holy Spirit. If you forgive the sins of any, they are forgiven; if you retain the sins of any, they are retained'" (Jn 20:21-23).

During his homily, John Paul also made clear that the Image of The Divine Mercy St. Faustina saw, which is to be venerated on Mercy Sunday, represents the Risen Christ bringing mercy to the world. (See *Diary,* 49, 88, 299, 341, 570, 742.) Pope John Paul II said: "Jesus shows His hands and His side [to the Apostles]. He points, that is, to the wounds of the Passion, especially the wound in His Heart, the source from which flows the great wave of mercy poured out on humanity.

"From that Heart, Sr. Faustina Kowalska, the blessed whom from now on we will call a saint, will see two rays of light shining from that Heart and illuminating the world: **The two** rays, Jesus Himself explained to her one day, **represent blood and water** *(Diary,* 299).

"Blood and water! We immediately think of the testimony given by the Evangelist John, who, when a soldier on Calvary pierced Christ's side with his spear, sees blood and water flowing from it (see Jn 19:34). Moreover, if the blood recalls the sacrifice of the cross and the gift of the Eucharist, the water, in Johannine symbolism, represents not only Baptism but also the gift of the Holy Spirit." (See Jn 3:5; 4:14; 7:37-39.)

From this teaching of Pope John Paul II on that most solemn occasion of the canonization of St. Faustina, it can be deduced that the most appropriate time for the solemn honoring of The Divine Mercy falls immediately after the Paschal Feast of Easter.

In fact, this is fully in accord with liturgical tradition. St. Augustine called the *eight days of Easter,* referring to the Octave, "days of mercy and pardon." Liturgically, these days constitute *a single day or a single celebration.* In a sermon, he then calls the Sunday of this Octave of Easter "the summary of the days of mercy."

It is no wonder, then, that already during his pilgrimage to [St.] Faustina's tomb on June 7, 1997, Pope John Paul II declared: "I give thanks to Divine Providence that I have been enabled to contribute personally to

57

the fulfillment of Christ's will through the institution of the Feast of Divine Mercy." He was referring to his approval for Mercy Sunday to be celebrated throughout Poland; now it is being celebrated as a universal feast with his blessing.

Veneration of the Image

The Image of Jesus, The Divine Mercy, is to have a special place of honor on the Feast of Mercy, a visual reminder of all that Jesus did for us through His Passion, Death, and Resurrection ... and a reminder, too, of what He asks of us in return — to trust Him and be merciful to others:

I want the Image to be solemnly blessed on the first Sunday after Easter, and I want it to be venerated publicly so that every soul may know about it *(Diary, 341).*

A group of the faithful celebrate Mercy Sunday at the National Shrine of The Divine Mercy in Stockbridge, MA, on April 30, 2000, the day St. Faustina was canonized.

A Special Promise of Mercy

Our Lord's promise to grant complete forgiveness of sins and punishment on the Feast of Mercy is recorded three times in the *Diary of St. Faustina,* each time in a slightly different way:

I want to grant a complete pardon to the souls that will go to Confession and receive Holy Communion on the Feast of My mercy (1109).

Whoever approaches the Fountain of Life on this day will be granted complete forgiveness of sins and punishment (300).

The soul that will go to Confession and receive Holy Communion will obtain complete forgiveness of sins and punishment (699).

Extraordinary Graces

Our Lord is also emphasizing, through this promise, the infinite value of Confession and Communion as miracles of mercy. He wants us to realize that since the Eucharist is His own Body, Blood, Soul, and Divinity, it *is* the "Fountain of Life" *(Diary,* 300). The Eucharist is Jesus, Himself, the Living God, longing to pour Himself as Mercy into our hearts.

Why would Our Lord feel the need to emphasize this? Because so many people do not really understand it. They either see no need to receive Holy Communion, or they receive it simply out of habit. As St. Paul explains in his letter to the Corinthians, they eat the bread or drink the cup of the Lord unworthily, "without recognizing the body of the Lord" (1 Cor 11:27-29).

In His revelations to St. Faustina Our Lord makes it very clear what He is offering us in Holy Communion and how much it hurts Him when we treat His presence with indifference:

My great delight is to unite Myself with souls. ... [W]hen I come to a human heart in Holy Communion, My hands are full of all kinds of graces which I want to give to the soul. But souls do not even pay any attention to Me; they leave Me to Myself and busy themselves with other things. Oh, how sad I am that souls do not recognize Love! They treat Me as a dead object (1385; also see 1288 and 1447).

So, Our Lord's promise of complete forgiveness is both a reminder and a call. It is a reminder that He is *truly present* and *truly alive* in the Eucharist, filled with love for us and waiting for us to turn to Him with trust. And it is a call for us *all* to be washed clean in His Love through Confession and Holy Communion — no matter how terrible our sins — and begin our lives again. He is offering us a new start.

Prepare Yourself Properly

Going to Confession is not the only way we should prepare ourselves for Divine Mercy Sunday. As Cardinal Francis Macharski, then Archbishop of Cracow,

Poland, explains in a 1985 pastoral letter, we are not simply called to ask for God's mercy with trust. We are also called to *be* merciful:

"Our own merciful attitude is likewise a preparation. Without deeds of mercy, our devotion would not be real. For Christ does not only reveal the mercy of God, but at the same time He places before people the demand that they conduct themselves in life with love and mercy. Pope John Paul II states that this requirement constitutes the very heart of the Gospel ethos *(Rich in Mercy,* 3) — it is the commandment of love and the promise: 'Blessed are the merciful, for they shall obtain mercy' (Mt 5:7). Let it be a mercy that is forgiving and true, and universal, with good words, deeds, and prayer for others!"

Our Lord's words to St. Faustina about this requirement to be merciful are very strong and leave no room for misinterpretation:

Yes, the first Sunday after Easter is the Feast of Mercy, but there must also be acts of mercy. ... I demand from you deeds of mercy, which are to arise out of love for Me. You are to show mercy to your neighbors always and everywhere. You must not shrink from this or try to excuse or absolve yourself from it (742).

Thus, to fittingly observe the Feast of Mercy, we should:

1. Celebrate the Feast on the Sunday after Easter;

2. Sincerely repent of all our sins;

3. Place our complete trust in Jesus;

4. Go to Confession, preferably before that Sunday;

5. Receive Holy Communion on the day of the Feast;

6. Venerate* the Image of The Divine Mercy;

7. Be merciful to others, through our actions, words, and prayers on their behalf.

*To venerate a sacred image or statue simply means to perform some act or make some gesture of deep religious respect toward it because of the person whom it represents — in this case, our Most Merciful Savior.

Thousands of pilgrims celebrate Mercy Sunday each year on Eden Hill in Stockbridge, MA.

The Chaplet of Divine Mercy

In 1935, St. Faustina received a vision of an angel sent by God to chastise a certain city. She began to pray for mercy, but her prayers were powerless. Suddenly she saw the Holy Trinity and felt the power of Jesus' grace within her. At the same time she found herself pleading with God for mercy with words she heard interiorly:

Eternal Father, I offer You the Body and Blood, Soul and Divinity of Your dearly beloved Son, Our Lord Jesus Christ, in atonement for our sins and those of the whole world; for the sake of His sorrowful Passion, have mercy on us (*Diary,* 475).

As she continued saying this inspired prayer, the angel became helpless and could not carry out the deserved punishment (see 474, 475).

The next day, as she was entering the chapel, she again heard this interior voice, instructing her how to recite the prayer that our Lord later called "the Chaplet." This time, after **have mercy on us** were added the words **and on the whole world** (476). From then on, she recited this form of prayer almost constantly, offering it especially for the dying.

In subsequent revelations, the Lord made it clear that the Chaplet was not just for her, but for the whole world. He also attached extraordinary promises to its recitation.

Encourage souls to say the Chaplet which I have given you (1541). **Whoever will recite it will receive great mercy at the hour of death** (687). **When they say this chaplet in the presence of the dying, I will stand between My Father and the dying person, not as the just Judge but as the Merciful Savior (1541). Priests will recommend it to sinners as their last hope of salvation. Even if there were a sinner most hardened, if he were to recite this chaplet only once, he would receive grace from My infinite mercy (687). I desire to grant unimaginable graces to those souls who trust in My mercy (687). Through the Chaplet you will obtain everything, if what you ask for is compatible with My will (1731).**

Prayed on ordinary rosary beads, the Chaplet of Divine Mercy is an intercessory prayer that extends the offering of the Eucharist, so it is especially appropriate to use it after having received Holy Communion at Holy Mass. It may be said at any time, but our Lord specifically told St. Faustina to recite it during the nine days before the Feast of Mercy (the first Sunday after Easter). He then added:

By this Novena, [of Chaplets] **I will grant every possible grace to souls** (796).

It is likewise appropriate to pray the Chaplet during the "Hour of Great Mercy" — three o'clock each afternoon (recalling the time of Christ's death on the cross).

In His revelations to St. Faustina, Our Lord asked for a special remembrance of His Passion at that hour. [See pages 72-73.]

The Chaplet can also be sung using various melodies, such as the one on page 60 of this booklet.

How to Recite the Chaplet

(On ordinary rosary beads)   *(Diary,* 476)

The Our Father

Our Father, Who art in heaven, hallowed be Thy name; Thy kingdom come; Thy will be done on earth as it is in heaven. Give us this day our daily bread; and forgive us our trespasses as we forgive those who trespass against us; and lead us not into temptation, but deliver us from evil. Amen.

The Hail Mary

Hail Mary, full of grace. The Lord is with thee. Blessed art thou among women, and blessed is the fruit of thy womb, Jesus. Holy Mary, Mother of God, pray for us sinners, now and at the hour of our death. Amen.

The Apostles' Creed

(Text from official approved translation. See Holy Saturday Liturgy in the Roman Missal.)

I believe in God, the Father almighty, creator of heaven and earth.

I believe in Jesus Christ, His only Son, our Lord. He was conceived by the power of the Holy Spirit, and born of the Virgin Mary. He suffered under Pontius Pilate, was crucified, died, and was buried. He descended to the dead. On the third day He rose again. He ascended into heaven, and is seated at the right hand of the Father. He will come again to judge the living and the dead.

I believe in the Holy Spirit, the holy catholic Church, the communion of saints, the forgiveness of sins, the resurrection of the body, and the life everlasting. Amen.

On the Our Father Bead before Each Decade:

Eternal Father,
I offer You
the Body and Blood,
Soul and Divinity
of Your dearly beloved Son,
Our Lord Jesus Christ,
in atonement for our sins
and those of the whole world.

On the 10 Hail Mary Beads of Each Decade:

For the sake of His sorrowful Passion,
have mercy on us
and on the whole world.

Concluding Doxology: (after five decades)

Holy God,
Holy Mighty One,
Holy Immortal One,
have mercy on us
and on the whole world.

(Three times)
Optional Concluding Prayer

Eternal God, in whom mercy is endless and the treasury of compassion inexhaustible, look kindly upon us and increase Your mercy in us, that in difficult moments we might not despair nor become despondent, but with great confidence submit ourselves to Your holy will, which is Love and Mercy itself (950).

How to Sing the Chaplet

Music by Marie Smetkiewicz

Adapted by Archb. G. H. Pearce, S.M.
and G. Farrell, M. M.

Begin with: *Our Father ..., Hail Mary.., I believe in God ...*
On the single beads, in place of the *Our Father:*

68

The Novena to The Divine Mercy

On Good Friday, 1937, Jesus requested that St. Faustina make a special novena before the Feast of Mercy, from Good Friday through the following Saturday. He, Himself, dictated the intentions for each day. By means of a specific prayer she was to bring to His Heart a different group of souls each day and thus immerse them in the ocean of His mercy, begging the Father — on the strength of Jesus' Passion — for graces for them. (See *Diary,* 1209.)

Unlike the Novena of Chaplets, which Our Lord clearly wants everyone to use [see pages 56-57], this second novena seems to have been intended primarily for St. Faustina's personal use. This can be seen from Our Lord's instructions, which address her with the word "you" in the singular.

But, since St. Faustina was commanded to write it down, Our Lord must have intended the Novena to be used by others, too. Once published, it immediately became very popular, and people prayed the Novena, not only in preparation for the Feast of Mercy, but at other times as well.

The wide range of intentions, which do not include personal needs, makes the great popularity of this novena all the more astounding. In this novena, we truly make the Lord's intentions our own — a beautiful expression of the Church's privilege and duty, as the Bride of the Lord, to

be the intercessor at Christ's side on the throne of mercy.
[The Novena begins on the next page.]

Prayers for the Novena
(Diary, 1209-1229)

It is greatly recommended that the following novena intentions and prayers be said together with the Chaplet of Divine Mercy, since Our Lord specifically asked for a novena of Chaplets, especially before the Feast of Mercy. [The Chaplet may be found on pages 58-59 of this booklet.]

First Day

Today bring to Me
ALL MANKIND, ESPECIALLY
ALL SINNERS,

and immerse them in the ocean of My mercy. In this way you will console Me in the bitter grief into which the loss of souls plunges Me.

Most Merciful Jesus, whose very nature it is to have compassion on us and to forgive us, do not look upon our sins but upon our trust which we place in Your infinite goodness. Receive us all into the abode of Your Most Compassionate Heart, and never let us escape from It. We beg this of You by Your love which unites You to the Father and the Holy Spirit.

Eternal Father, turn Your merciful gaze upon all mankind and especially upon poor sinners, all enfolded in the Most Compassionate Heart of Jesus. For the sake of His sorrowful Passion show us Your mercy, that we may praise the omnipotence of Your mercy forever and ever. Amen.

Second Day

Today bring to Me
THE SOULS OF PRIESTS AND RELIGIOUS,

and immerse them in My unfathomable mercy. It was they who gave Me strength to endure My bitter Passion. Through them as through channels My mercy flows out upon mankind.

Most Merciful Jesus, from whom comes all that is good, increase Your grace in men and women consecrated to Your service,* that they may perform worthy works of mercy; and that all who see them may glorify the Father of Mercy who is in heaven.

Eternal Father, turn Your merciful gaze upon the company of chosen ones in Your vineyard — upon the souls of priests and religious; and endow them with the strength of Your blessing. For the love of the Heart of Your Son in which they are enfolded, impart to them Your power and light, that they may be able to guide others in the way of salvation and with one voice sing praise to Your boundless mercy for ages without end. Amen.

* In the original text, St. Faustina uses the pronoun "us" since she was offering this prayer as a consecrated religious sister. The wording adapted here is intended to make the prayer suitable for universal use.

Third Day

Today bring to Me
ALL DEVOUT AND FAITHFUL SOULS,

and immerse them in the ocean of My mercy. These souls brought Me consolation on the Way of the Cross. They were that drop of consolation in the midst of an ocean of bitterness. Most Merciful Jesus, from the treasury of Your mercy, You impart Your graces in great abundance to each and all. Receive us into the abode of Your Most Compassionate Heart and never let us escape from It. We beg this grace of You by that most wondrous love for the heavenly Father with which Your Heart burns so fiercely.

Eternal Father, turn Your merciful gaze upon faithful souls, as upon the inheritance of Your Son. For the sake of His sorrowful Passion, grant them Your blessing and surround them with Your constant protection. Thus may they never fail in love or lose the treasure of the holy faith, but rather, with all the hosts of Angels and Saints, may they glorify Your boundless mercy for endless ages. Amen.

Fourth Day

Today bring to Me
THOSE WHO DO NOT BELIEVE IN GOD*
AND THOSE WHO DO NOT YET KNOW ME.

I was thinking also of them during My bitter Passion, and their future zeal comforted My Heart. Immerse them in the ocean of My mercy.

Most compassionate Jesus, You are the Light of the

whole world. Receive into the abode of Your Most Compassionate Heart the souls of those who do not believe in God and of those who as yet do not know You. Let the rays of Your grace enlighten them that they, too, together with us, may extol Your wonderful mercy; and do not let them escape from the abode which is Your Most Compassionate Heart.

Eternal Father, turn Your merciful gaze upon the souls of those who do not believe in You, and of those who as yet do not know You, but who are enclosed in the Most Compassionate Heart of Jesus. Draw them to the light of the Gospel. These souls do not know what great happiness it is to love You. Grant that they, too, may extol the generosity of Your mercy for endless ages. Amen.

* Our Lord's original words here were "the pagans." Since the pontificate of Pope John XXIII, the Church has seen fit to replace this term with clearer and more appropriate terminology.

Fifth Day

Today bring to Me
THE SOULS OF THOSE WHO HAVE SEPARATED THEMSELVES FROM MY CHURCH,*

and immerse them in the ocean of My mercy. During My bitter Passion they tore at My Body and Heart, that is, My Church. As they return to unity with the Church My wounds heal and in this way they alleviate My Passion.

Most Merciful Jesus, Goodness Itself, You do not refuse light to those who seek it of You. Receive into the abode of Your Most Compassionate Heart the souls of

73

those who have separated themselves from Your Church. Draw them by Your light into the unity of the Church, and do not let them escape from the abode of Your Most Compassionate Heart; but bring it about that they, too, come to glorify the generosity of Your mercy.

Eternal Father, turn Your merciful gaze upon the souls of those who have separated themselves from Your Son's Church, who have squandered Your blessings and misused Your graces by obstinately persisting in their errors. Do not look upon their errors, but upon the love of Your own Son and upon His bitter Passion, which He underwent for their sake, since they, too, are enclosed in His Most Compassionate Heart. Bring it about that they also may glorify Your great mercy for endless ages. Amen.

* Our Lord's original words here were "heretics and schismatics," since He spoke to St. Faustina within the context of her times. As of the Second Vatican Council, Church authorities have seen fit not to use those designations in accordance with the explanation given in the Council's Decree on Ecumenism (n.3). Every pope since the Council has reaffirmed that usage. St. Faustina herself, her heart always in harmony with the mind of the Church, most certainly would have agreed. When at one time, because of the decisions of her superiors and father confessor, she was not able to execute Our Lord's inspirations and orders, she declared: "I will follow Your will insofar as You will permit me to do so through Your representative. O my Jesus, I give priority to the voice of the Church over the voice with which You speak to me" *(Diary, 497)*. The Lord confirmed her action and praised her for it.

Sixth Day

Today bring to Me
THE MEEK AND HUMBLE SOULS AND
THE SOULS OF LITTLE CHILDREN,

and immerse them in My mercy. These souls most closely resemble My Heart. They strengthened Me during My bitter agony. I saw them as earthly Angels, who will keep

vigil at My altars. I pour out upon them whole torrents of grace. Only the humble soul is capable of receiving My grace. I favor humble souls with My confidence.

Most Merciful Jesus, You yourself have said, "Learn from Me for I am meek and humble of heart." Receive into the abode of Your Most Compassionate Heart all meek and humble souls and the souls of little children. These souls send all heaven into ecstasy and they are the heavenly Father's favorites. They are a sweet-smelling bouquet before the throne of God; God himself takes delight in their fragrance. These souls have a permanent abode in Your Most Compassionate Heart, O Jesus, and they unceasingly sing out a hymn of love and mercy.

Eternal Father, turn Your merciful gaze upon meek souls, upon humble souls, and upon little children who are enfolded in the abode which is the Most Compassionate Heart of Jesus. These souls bear the closest resemblance to Your Son. Their fragrance rises from the earth and reaches Your very throne. Father of mercy and of all goodness, I beg You by the love You bear these souls and by the delight You take in them: Bless the whole world, that all souls together may sing out the praises of Your mercy for endless ages. Amen.

Seventh Day

Today bring to Me
THE SOULS WHO ESPECIALLY VENERATE AND GLORIFY MY MERCY, *

and immerse them in My mercy. These souls sorrowed

most over my Passion and entered most deeply into My spirit. They are living images of My Compassionate Heart. These souls will shine with a special brightness in the next life. Not one of them will go into the fire of hell. I shall particularly defend each one of them at the hour of death.

Most Merciful Jesus, whose Heart is Love Itself, receive into the abode of Your Most Compassionate Heart the souls of those who particularly extol and venerate the greatness of Your mercy. These souls are mighty with the very power of God Himself. In the midst of all afflictions and adversities they go forward, confident of Your mercy; and united to You, O Jesus, they carry all mankind on their shoulders. These souls will not be judged severely, but Your mercy will embrace them as they depart from this life.

Eternal Father, turn Your merciful gaze upon the souls who glorify and venerate Your greatest attribute, that of Your fathomless mercy, and who are enclosed in the Most Compassionate Heart of Jesus. These souls are a living Gospel; their hands are full of deeds of mercy, and their hearts, overflowing with joy, sing a canticle of mercy to You, O Most High! I beg You O God: Show them Your mercy according to the hope and trust they have placed in You. Let there be accomplished in them the promise of Jesus, who said to them that during their life, but especially at the hour of death, the souls who will venerate this fathomless mercy of His, He, Himself, will defend as His glory. Amen.

* The text leads one to conclude that in the first prayer directed to Jesus, who is the Redeemer, it is "victim" souls and contemplatives that are being prayed

for; those persons, that is, that voluntarily offered themselves to God for the salvation of their neighbor (see Col 1:24; 2 Cor 4:12). This explains their close union with the Savior and the extraordinary efficacy that their invisible activity has for others. In the second prayer, directed to the Father from whom comes "every worthwhile gift and every genuine benefit," we recommend the "active" souls, who promote devotion to The Divine Mercy and exercise with it all the other works that lend themselves to the spiritual and material uplifting of their brethren.

Eighth Day

Today bring to Me
THE SOULS WHO ARE DETAINED
IN PURGATORY,

and immerse them in the abyss of My mercy. Let the torrents of My Blood cool down their scorching flames. All these souls are greatly loved by Me. They are making retribution to My justice. It is in your power to bring them relief. Draw all the indulgences from the treasury of My Church and offer them on their behalf. Oh, if you only knew the torments they suffer, you would continually offer for them the alms of the spirit and pay off their debt to My justice.

Most Merciful Jesus, You Yourself have said that You desire mercy; so I bring into the abode of Your Most Compassionate Heart the souls in Purgatory, souls who are very dear to You, and yet, who must make retribution to Your justice. May the streams of Blood and Water which gushed forth from Your Heart put out the flames of Purgatory, that there, too, the power of Your mercy may be celebrated.

Eternal Father, turn Your merciful gaze upon the souls suffering in Purgatory, who are enfolded in the Most

Compassionate Heart of Jesus. I beg You, by the sorrowful Passion of Jesus Your Son, and by all the bitterness with which His most sacred Soul was flooded: Manifest Your mercy to the souls who are under Your just scrutiny. Look upon them in no other way but only through the Wounds of Jesus, Your dearly beloved Son; for we firmly believe that there is no limit to Your goodness and compassion. Amen.

Ninth Day

Today bring to Me
SOULS WHO HAVE BECOME LUKEWARM,*

and immerse them in the abyss of My mercy. These souls wound My Heart most painfully. My soul suffered the most dreadful loathing in the Garden of Olives because of lukewarm souls. They were the reason I cried out: "Father, take this cup away from Me, if it be Your will." For them the last hope of salvation is to run to My mercy.

Most compassionate Jesus, You are Compassion Itself. I bring lukewarm souls into the abode of Your Most Compassionate Heart. In this fire of Your pure love let these tepid souls, who, like corpses, filled You with such deep loathing, be once again set aflame. O Most Compassionate Jesus, exercise the omnipotence of Your mercy and draw them into the very ardor of Your love, and bestow upon them the gift of holy love, for nothing is beyond Your power.

Eternal Father, turn Your merciful gaze upon luke-warm souls who are nonetheless enfolded in the Most Compassionate Heart of Jesus. Father of Mercy, I beg You by the bitter Passion of Your Son and by His three-hour agony on the Cross: Let them, too, glorify the abyss of Your mercy. Amen.

* To understand who are the souls designated for this day, and who in the Diary are called "lukewarm," but are also compared to ice and to corpses, we would do well to take note of the definition that the Savior Himself gave them when speaking to St. Faustina about them on one occasion: **There are souls who thwart My efforts (1682). Souls without love or devotion, souls full of ego-ism and selfishness, proud and arrogant souls full of deceit and hypocrisy, lukewarm souls who have just enough warmth to keep themselves alive: My Heart cannot bear this. All the graces that I pour out upon them flow off them as off the face of a rock. I cannot stand them because they are neither good nor bad (1702).**

The Hour of Great Mercy

In His revelations to St. Faustina, Our Lord asked for special prayer and meditation on His Passion each afternoon at the three o'clock hour, the hour that recalls His death on the cross.

At three o'clock, implore My mercy, especially for sinners; and, if only for a brief moment, immerse yourself in My Passion, particularly in My abandon-ment at the moment of agony. This is the hour of great mercy.... In this hour I will refuse nothing to the soul that makes a request of Me in virtue of My Passion (*Diary,* 1320).

As often as you hear the clock strike the third hour, immerse yourself completely in My mercy, adoring and glorifying it; invoke its omnipotence for the whole world, and particularly for poor sinners; for at that moment mercy was opened wide for every soul. In this hour you can obtain everything for yourself and for others for the asking; it was the hour of grace for the whole world — mercy triumphed over justice....

My daughter, try your best to make the Stations of the Cross in this hour, provided that your duties permit it; and if you are not able to make the Stations of the Cross, then at least step into the chapel for a moment and adore, in the Most Blessed Sacrament, My Heart, which is full of mercy; and should you be unable to step into chapel, immerse yourself in prayer there where you happen to be, if only for a very brief instant (1572).

From these detailed instructions, it's clear that Our Lord wants us to turn our attention to His Passion at the three o'clock hour to whatever degree our duties allow, and He wants us to ask for His mercy.

In *Genesis* 18:16-32, Abraham begged God to reduce the conditions necessary for Him to be merciful to the people of Sodom and Gomorrah. Here, Christ Himself offers a reduction of conditions because of the varied demands of our life's duties, and *He begs us* to ask, even in the smallest way, for His mercy, so that He will be able to pour His mercy upon us all.

We may not all be able to make the Stations or adore Him in the Blessed Sacrament, but we can all mentally pause for a "brief instant," think of His total abandonment at the hour of agony, and say a short prayer such as "Jesus, Mercy," or "Jesus, for the sake of Your Sorrowful Passion, have mercy on us and on the whole world."

This meditation, however brief, on Christ's Passion brings us face-to-face with the cross, and, as Pope John Paul II writes in *Rich in Mercy,* "It is in the cross that the revelation of merciful love attains its culmination" (8). God invites us, the Holy Father continues, "to have 'mercy' on His only Son, the crucified one" (8). Thus, our reflection on the Passion should lead to a type of love for Our Lord which is "not only an act of solidarity with the suffering Son of man, but also a kind of 'mercy' shown by each one of us to the Son of the Eternal Father" (8). [See the next page of this booklet for Mercy Stations appropriate for use at the three o'clock hour.]

Mercy Stations *

Begin each station with:

Eternal Father, I offer You the Body and Blood, Soul and Divinity of Your dearly beloved Son, Our Lord Jesus Christ, in atonement for our sins and those of the whole world.

Pause briefly, meditating on the Passion of Jesus.

Then say the invocation given below, followed by: **have mercy on us and on the whole world.**

Invocations

1. For the sake of His institution of the Eucharist as the memorial of His Passion, ...
2. For the sake of His agony in the Garden, ...
3. For the sake of His being scourged and crowned with thorns, ...
4. For the sake of His being condemned to death,...
5. For the sake of His carrying the Cross, ...
6. For the sake of His falling under the weight of the cross, ...
7. For the sake of His meeting His afflicted Mother, ...
8. For the sake of His accepting help in carrying the Cross,...
9. For the sake of His receiving mercy from Veronica, ...
10. For the sake of His consoling the women, ...
11. For the sake of His being stripped, ...
12. For the sake of His being crucified, ...
13. For the sake of His death on the Cross, ...
14. For the sake of His being buried, ...
15. For the sake of His being raised from the dead,...

Holy God, Holy Mighty One, Holy Immortal One, Have mercy on us and on the whole world.

(three times)

* These stations do not follow the traditional set found in churches.

Living the Message of Mercy

The devotional practices revealed through St. Faustina were given to us as "vessels of mercy" through which God's love can be poured out upon the world, but they are not sufficient unto themselves. It's not enough for us to hang The Divine Mercy Image in our homes, pray the Chaplet every day at three o'clock, and receive Holy Communion on the first Sunday after Easter. We also have to show mercy to our neighbors. *Putting mercy into action is not an option of the Divine Mercy message and devotion; it's a requirement!*

How strongly Our Lord speaks about this to St. Faustina!

I *demand* from you *deeds of mercy* which are to arise out of love for me. *You are to show mercy to your neighbors always and everywhere.* You must not shrink from this or try to excuse yourself from it *(Diary, 742).*

Like the Gospel command, "Be merciful, just as your Father is merciful," this demand that we show mercy to our neighbors "always and everywhere" seems impossible to fulfill. But the Lord assures us that it is possible. **When a soul approaches Me with trust,** He explains, **I fill it with such an abundance of graces that it cannot contain them within itself, but radiates them to other souls** (1074).

How do we "radiate" God's mercy to others? By our *actions,* our *words,* and our *prayers.* **In these three de-**

grees, He tells St. Faustina, **is contained the fullness of mercy**

(742). We have all been called to this threefold practice of mercy, but we are not all called in the same way. We need to ask the Lord, who understands our individual personalities and situations, to help us recognize the various ways we can each live His mercy in our daily lives.

One thing we can *all* do is take a fresh look at what the Church calls the Spiritual and Corporal Works of Mercy, a list of 14 ways to respond to the physical, mental, emotional, and spiritual needs of others. [See inside front cover.]

Saint Faustina herself learned that when she practiced the works of mercy, she was actually serving the merciful Savior Himself: "As you did it to one of the least of these My brethren, you did to Me" (Mt 25:35-40). The Lord's compassion flowed through her to the materially and spiritually poor, because she recognized that they were most in need of His mercy.

She never forgot how a poor young man, barefoot and with his clothes in tatters, came to her convent gate on a cold and rainy day begging for hot food. She immediately went to the kitchen, but found nothing there for him. Sister Faustina finally succeeded in finding some soup, which she reheated and into which she crumbled some bread. After the young man ate the soup, He unveiled to her His true identity — the Lord Jesus Christ Himself!

Then he vanished from her sight. But, later, she heard these words in her soul:

My **daughter, the blessings of the poor who bless Me as they leave this gate have reached My ears. And your compassion, within the bounds of obedience, has pleased Me, and this is why I came down from My throne — to taste the fruits of your mercy** *(Diary,* 1312).

Mercy for the Dying

One of the greatest works of mercy we can perform — and one often overlooked — is to pray for the dying. For St. Faustina, this was an important aspect of her mission of mercy. "Oh, dying souls are in such need of prayer," St. Faustina wrote in her *Diary.* "O Jesus, inspire souls to pray often for the dying" (1015).

The Lord Himself impressed upon her the importance of such prayers when He said to her:

Pray as much as you can for the dying. By your entreaties, obtain for them trust in My mercy, because they have most need of trust, and have it the least. Be assured that the grace of eternal salvation for certain souls in their final moments depends on your prayer (1777).

In particular, Jesus recommended to St. Faustina to use the Chaplet to aid the dying: **At the hour of their death, I defend as My own glory every soul that will say this Chaplet; or when others say it for a dying person, the indulgence** [pardon] **is the same** (811).

When we pray for the dying in this way, we can be

assured that it opens the floodgates of Divine Mercy for souls in their time of greatest weakness and greatest need: "God's mercy sometimes touches the sinner at the last moment in a wondrous and mysterious way. Outwardly, it seems as if everything were lost, but it is not so. The soul, illumined by a ray of God's powerful final grace, turns to God in the last moment with such a power of love that, in an instant, it receives from God forgiveness of sin and punishment ..." (1698).

Mercy for the Dead

Along with prayer for the dying, another great work of mercy is to pray for the dead. As the *Catechism of the Catholic Church* teaches:

"All who die in God's grace and friendship, but still imperfectly purified, are indeed assured of their eternal salvation; but after death they undergo purification, so as to achieve the holiness necessary to enter the joy of heaven" (1030).

Jesus Himself encouraged St. Faustina to remember the souls in purgatory. He told her: **Enter into purgatory often, because** [souls] **need you there** (*Diary,* 1738). One time St. Faustina saw in a vision the souls suffering in purgatory, and she saw their great need for our assistance: "I saw my Guardian Angel, who ordered me to follow him. In a moment, I was in a misty place full of fire in which there was a great crowd of suffering souls. They were praying fervently, but to no avail, for themselves; only we can come to their aid. The flames which were burning them did not touch me at all. My Guardian Angel did not leave me for an instant. I asked these souls what their greatest suffering was. They answered me in one voice that their greatest torment was longing for God. I saw Our Lady visiting the souls in purgatory. The souls call her 'The Star of the Sea.' She brings them refreshment. ... Since that time, I am in closer communion with the suffering souls" (20).

Preparing for the Second Coming

Our Lord makes it very clear to St. Faustina that this need to proclaim His message of mercy is urgent, because the world needs it as a preparation for His coming again:

Speak to the world about My mercy. ... It is a sign for the end times;* after it will come the Day of Justice (*Diary,* 848). **You will prepare the world for My final coming (429). [T]ell souls about this great mercy of Mine, because the awful day, the day of My justice, is near** (965).

Repeatedly the Lord tells St. Faustina that He is offering sinners the "last hope of salvation." No matter how great our sins, He wants us to come back to Him, but we must respond now, while it is still the time of mercy:

Before the Day of Justice, I am sending the Day of Mercy (1588). I am prolonging the time of mercy for the sake of sinners. But woe to them if they do

not recognize this time of My visitation (1160). While there is still time, let them have recourse to the fount of My mercy (848). He who refuses to pass through the door of My mercy must pass through the door of My justice (1146).

Our Lady, too, speaks to St. Faustina about the urgency of the message of mercy:

[Y]ou have to speak to the world about His great mercy and prepare the world for the Second Coming of Him who will come, not as a merciful Savior, but as a just Judge. Oh how terrible is that day! Determined is the day of justice, the day of divine wrath. The angels tremble before it. Speak to souls about this great mercy while it is still the time for granting mercy (635).

Pope John Paul II seemed to have a strong sense of this urgency. In 1981, at the Shrine of Merciful Love in Collevalenza, Italy, he stated that from the very beginning of his ministry he has considered spreading the message of mercy as his "special task," assigned to him by God "in the present situation of man, the Church, and the world." In four of his encyclicals, he stresses that we are now living in a special time of preparation for the new coming of the Lord. He urges us "to implore God's mercy for humanity in this hour of history ... to beg for it at this difficult, critical phase of the history of the Church and of the world" *(Rich in Mercy,* 15).

* The "end times" began with the descent of the Holy Spirit and the birth of the Church.

SELECTED PRAYERS
FROM THE DIARY

Little Prayers for Use at the Hour of Great Mercy

You expired Jesus, but the source of life gushed forth for souls, and the ocean of mercy opened up for the whole world. O Fount of Life, unfathomable Divine Mercy, envelop the whole world and empty Yourself out upon us (1319).

O Blood and Water which gushed forth from the Heart of Jesus as a fount of mercy for us, I trust in You (84).

At the Feet of Christ in the Eucharist

O Jesus, Divine Prisoner of Love, when I consider Your love and how You emptied Yourself for me, my senses fail me. You hide Your inconceivable majesty and lower Yourself to miserable me. O King of Glory, though You hide Your beauty, yet the eye of my soul rends the veil. I see the angelic choirs giving You honor without cease, and all the heavenly Powers praising You without cease, and without cease they are saying: Holy, Holy, Holy.

Oh, who will comprehend Your love and Your unfathomable mercy toward us! O Prisoner of Love, I lock up my poor heart in this tabernacle that it may adore You without cease night and day. I know of no obstacle in this adoration, and even though I be physically distant, my heart is always with You. Nothing can put a stop to my love for You. No obstacles exist for me (80).

O Holy Trinity, One and Indivisible God, may You be blessed for this great gift and testament of mercy (81).

I adore You, Lord and Creator, hidden in the Blessed Sacrament. I adore You for all the works of Your hands, that reveal to me so much wisdom, goodness and mercy, O Lord. You have spread so much beauty over the earth, and it tells me about Your beauty, even though these beautiful things are but a faint reflection of You, Incomprehensible Beauty. And although You have hidden Yourself and concealed Your beauty, my eye, enlightened by faith, reaches You, and my soul recognizes its Creator, its Highest Good; and my heart is completely immersed in prayer of adoration (1692).

My Lord and Creator, Your goodness encourages me to converse with You. Your mercy abolishes the chasm which separates the Creator from the creature. To converse with You, O Lord, is the delight of my heart. In You I find everything that my heart could desire. Here Your light illumines my mind, enabling it to know You more and more deeply. Here streams of graces flow down upon my heart. Here my soul draws eternal life. O my Lord and Creator, You alone, beyond all these gifts, give Your own self to me and unite Yourself intimately with Your miserable creature (1692).

O Christ, I am most delighted when I see that You are loved, and that Your praise and glory resound, especially the praise of Your mercy. O Christ, to the last moment of my life, I will not stop glorifying Your goodness and mercy. With every drop of my blood, with every beat of my heart, I glorify Your mercy. I long to be entirely transformed into a hymn of Your glory. When I find myself on my deathbed, may the last beat of my heart be a loving hymn in praise of Your unfathomable mercy (1708).

Praises of The Divine Mercy
(948-949)
The Love of God is the flower—Mercy the fruit.

Let the doubting soul read these considerations on Divine Mercy and become trusting.

Divine Mercy, gushing forth from the bosom of the Father,
/ *Trust in You.*

Divine Mercy, greatest attribute of God,
/ *Trust in You.*

Divine Mercy, incomprehensible mystery,
/ *Trust in You.*

Divine Mercy, fountain gushing forth from the mystery of
the Most Blessed Trinity, / *Trust in You.*

Divine Mercy, unfathomed by any intellect, human or angelic,
/ *Trust in You.*

Divine Mercy, from which wells forth all life and happiness,
/ *Trust in You.*

Divine Mercy, better than the heavens,
/ *Trust in You.*

Divine Mercy, source of miracles and wonders,
/ *Trust in You.*

Divine Mercy, encompassing the whole universe,
/ *Trust in You.*

Divine Mercy, descending to earth in the Person of the
Incarnate Word,
/ *Trust in You.*

Divine Mercy, which flowed out from the open wound of the
Heart of Jesus,
/ *Trust in You.*

Divine Mercy, enclosed in the Heart of Jesus for us, and especially for sinners, / *Trust in You.*

Divine Mercy, unfathomed in the institution of the Sacred Host, / *Trust in You.*

Divine Mercy, in the founding of Holy Church, / *Trust in You.*

Divine Mercy, in the Sacrament of Holy Baptism, / *Trust in You.*

Divine Mercy, in our justification through Jesus Christ, / *Trust in You.*

Divine Mercy, accompanying us through our whole life, / *Trust in You.*

Divine Mercy, embracing us especially at the hour of death, / *Trust in You.*

Divine Mercy, endowing us with immortal life, / *Trust in You.*

Divine Mercy, accompanying us every moment of our life, / *Trust in You.*

Divine Mercy, shielding us from the fire of hell, / *Trust in You.*

Divine Mercy, in the conversion of hardened sinners, / *Trust in You.*

Divine Mercy, astonishment for Angels, incomprehensible to Saints, / *Trust in You.*

Divine Mercy, unfathomed in all the mysteries of God, / *Trust in You.*

Divine Mercy, lifting us out of every misery, / *Trust in You.*

Divine Mercy, source of our happiness and joy, / *Trust in You.*

Divine Mercy, in calling us forth from nothingness to existence, / *Trust in You.*

Divine Mercy, embracing all the works of His hands, / *Trust in You.*

Divine Mercy, crown of all of God's handiwork,
/ *Trust in You.*
Divine Mercy, in which we are all immersed, / *Trust in You.*
Divine Mercy, sweet relief for anguished hearts,
/ *Trust in You.*
Divine Mercy, only hope of despairing souls, / *Trust in You.*
Divine Mercy, repose of hearts, peace amidst fear,
/ *Trust in You.*
Divine Mercy, delight and ecstasy of holy souls,
/ *Trust in You.*
Divine Mercy, inspiring hope against all hope, / *Trust in You.*

To The Divine Mercy

I fly to Your mercy, Compassionate God, who alone are
good. Although my misery is great and my offenses are
many, I trust in Your mercy, because You are the God of
mercy; and, from time immemorial, it has never been heard
of, nor do heaven or earth remember, that a soul trusting in
Your mercy has been disappointed.

O God of compassion, You alone can justify me and You
will never reject me when I, contrite, approach Your Merciful Heart, where no one has ever been refused, even if
he were the greatest sinner (1730). [For Your Son assured
me:] **Sooner would heaven and earth turn into nothingness than would My mercy fail to embrace a trusting
soul** (1777).

Jesus, Friend of a lonely heart, You are my haven, You
are my peace. You are my salvation, You are my serenity in
moments of struggle and amidst an ocean of doubts. You
are the bright ray that lights up the path of my life. You are

everything to a lonely soul. You understand the soul even though it remains silent. You know our weaknesses and, like a good physician, You comfort and heal, sparing us sufferings — expert that You are (247).

In Thanksgiving

O Jesus, eternal God, I thank You for Your countless graces and blessings. Let every beat of my heart be a new hymn of thanksgiving to You, O God. Let every drop of my blood circulate for You, Lord. My soul is one hymn in adoration of Your mercy. I love You, God, for Yourself alone (1794).

Mother of Mercy (Ostra Brama Image) in Vilnius, Lithuania.

To the Mother of God

O Mary, my mother and my lady, I offer you my soul, my body, my life and my death, and all that will follow it. I place everything in your hands. O my mother, cover my soul with your virginal mantle and grant me the grace of purity of heart, soul and body. Defend me with your power against all enemies, and especially against those who hide their malice behind the mask of virtue (79). Fortify my soul that pain will not break it. Mother of grace, teach me to live by God's power (315).

O Mary ... a terrible sword has pierced your holy soul. Except for God, no one knows of your suffering. Your soul does not break; it is brave, because it is with Jesus. Sweet Mother, unite my soul to Jesus, because it is only then that I will be able to endure all trials and tribulations, and only in union with Jesus will my little sacrifices be pleasing to God. Sweetest Mother, continue to teach me about the interior life. May the sword of suffering never break me. O pure Virgin, pour courage into my heart and guard it (915).

For the Grace to Be Merciful to Others

This prayer gives us a true measure of our mercy, a mirror in which we observe ourselves as merciful Christs. We can make it our morning invocation and our evening examination of conscience.

O Most Holy Trinity! As many times as I breathe, as many times as my heart beats, as many times as my blood pulsates through my body, so many thousand times do I want to glorify Your mercy.

I want to be completely transformed into Your mercy and to be Your living reflection, O Lord. May the greatest of all divine attributes, that of Your unfathomable mercy, pass through my heart and soul to my neighbor.

Help me, O Lord, that my eyes may be merciful, so that I may never suspect or judge from appearances, but look for what is beautiful in my neighbors' souls and come to their rescue.

Help me, that my ears may be merciful, so that I may give heed to my neighbors' needs and not be indifferent to their pains and moanings.

Help me, O Lord, that my tongue may be merciful, so that I should never speak negatively of my neighbor, but have a word of comfort and forgiveness for all.

Help me, O Lord, that my hands may be merciful and filled with good deeds, so that I may do only good to my neighbors and take upon myself the more difficult and toilsome tasks.

Help me, that my feet may be merciful, so that I may hurry to assist my neighbor, overcoming my own fatigue and weariness. My true rest is in the service of my neighbor.

Help me, O Lord, that my heart may be merciful so that I myself may feel all the sufferings of my neighbor. I will refuse my heart to no one. I will be sincere even with those who, I know, will abuse my kindness. And I will lock myself up in the most merciful Heart of Jesus. I will bear my own suffering in silence. May Your mercy, O Lord, rest upon me.

You Yourself command me to exercise the three degrees of mercy. The first: the act of mercy, of whatever kind. The second: the word of mercy — if I cannot carry out a work of mercy, I will assist by my words. The third: prayer — if I cannot show mercy by deeds or words, I can always do so by prayer. My prayer reaches out even there where I cannot reach out physically.

O my Jesus, transform me into Yourself, for You can do all things (163).